How to Have an Attitude of Gratitude on the Night Shift

How to Have an Attitude of Gratitude on the Night Shift

Poetry: Teresa Flowers

Narration: Jeanne DeFazio

Introduction: William David Spencer

RESOURCE *Publications* • Eugene, Oregon

HOW TO HAVE AN ATTITUDE OF GRATITUDE ON THE NIGHT SHIFT

Copyright © 2014 Teresa Flowers, Jeanne DeFazio. All rights reserved. Except for brief quotations in critical publications or reviews, no part of this book may be reproduced in any manner without prior written permission from the publisher. Write: Permissions. Wipf and Stock Publishers, 199 W. 8th Ave., Suite 3, Eugene, OR 97401.

Resource Publications
An Imprint of Wipf and Stock Publishers
199 W. 8th Ave., Suite 3
Eugene, OR 97401

www.wipfandstock.com

ISBN 13: 978-1-4982-0776-8

Manufactured in the U.S.A.   12/15/2014

Table of Contents

Acknowledgments | vi
Introduction | vii

Listen to My Heartbeat | 1
Second Mile Walk | 2
The Kitchen Prayer | 3
Smell of God | 4
I Stood | 5
Lonely Night of the Soul | 6
God's Interpretations | 7
Make Them into Your Image, Make Them into Your Children | 8
Come to the Place | 9
Let Them Seek Your Face | 10
Morning Prayer | 11
Perfect Our Hearts | 12
Father of Their Souls | 13
When God's Children Pray | 14
Quietness of Souls, the Holy Spirit Moves over Them | 15
Bring the Light to the Darkness of Their Hearts | 16
Cause Them to Seek You with Their Hearts | 17
I Am Silent Before You | 18
Fire of the Lord | 19
Let the Children Come and Worship You | 20
Voice of the Holy Spirit, Speak Softly | 21
Your Touch Has Caressed Their Souls | 22
May the Blessings of the Lord Be upon the Children | 23
You Know | 24
On Eagles' Wings of Love | 25

Acknowledgments

To Abba Father, thank You for breathing in me the Holy Spirit, to write Your poems;

Aunt Esther, my Godmother, and my Uncle Tom, for being there for me;

Chris C., for nudging me to write;

Irene, Steven, Ceej, Olga, Sharon, Patrick, my friends and family;

Kemosabe, my faithful brother in Christ;

Sunshine, thank you for teaching me to pray, pray more, keep praying;

Doug, thank you for being my chariot driver;

Thanks to Caleb Loring III for his support of this project;

Many thanks to Suzanne Parada for her talent as a graphic artist that has made this book so special. We are indebted to her for her kindness;

Thanks to John Lathrop and Esmé Bieberly for their help with editing;

To my brothers and sisters at Pilgrim Church, for praying for me and with me;

Last but not least, to Jeanne D., for being the glue to this book;

You are loved.

—Teresa Two Feathers Flowers

Introduction

> Lord of all pots and pans and things . . . Make me a saint by getting meals and washing up the plates![1]

In a quest to find spiritual peace on a summer day in an August some three-and-a-half centuries ago, a powerful and influential ecclesiastical administrator, named M. Beaufort, who served as Grand Vicar to a Cardinal, stood in a rough and crude monastery kitchen. He was listening intently as "a great awkward fellow who broke everything" enlightened him on how "we should establish ourselves in a sense of God's presence by continually conversing with Him."

Brother Lawrence, as this simple but spiritually profound cook had come to be known, had discovered the meaning of the Apostle Paul's advice to the troubled church at Thessalonica[2] that all of us can thrive within difficult lives and perform the most challenging of jobs if we present each moment quietly to God, living out our lives and doing our jobs with a conscious sense that we are doing so in the presence of the caring and loving God who created us and everyone else, including those we serve.

Like Brother Lawrence, the poet whose words are chronicled in this book is a cook. Teresa "Two Feathers" Flowers, who hails from Amarillo, Texas, is of Cherokee and Lebanese/Dutch descent. Generally in public, she

---

1. Brother Lawrence, "A Pilgrim's Prayer." In *The Practice of the Presence of God with Spiritual Maxims* (Grand Rapids, MI: Spire, 1958), 9.

2. 1 Thessalonians 5:17: "Constantly pray!" Translation by author.

Introduction

is as silent as the desert on a starry night. Two Feathers speaks through her others-oriented actions and the economy of her poems. Whatever practical needs to be done, she does it. Currently, she is the elder who serves with the deacons of Pilgrim Church, a storefront mission church in the small city of Beverly, Massachusetts. Many Sundays, Two Feathers volunteers to cook a meal free to the public and consequently feeds a small army composed of anyone who drops in, using a budget (mainly provided by her) about the size of a one-family trip to McDonald's. Think of a cook on a cattle drive, gently soothing the calves, thoroughly nourishing the cowhands on a larder of next to nothing, devoutly communing with God on the high plains, and steadily persevering through rain and wind and snow and hail, ever calm, pleasant, constant, capable, and totally reliable. That's Two Feathers.

Brother Lawrence explained to his chronicler, "The time of business... does not with me differ from the time of prayer; and in the noise and clatter of my kitchen, while several persons are at the same time calling for different things, I possess God in as great tranquility as if I were upon my knees at the blessed sacrament."[3]

Like Brother Lawrence's life, Two Feathers's is a solitary one lived out in dedication and service to God and people. Widowed at a young age, she has dedicated her professional life to providing social services to at-risk children.

Brother Lawrence explained, "We can do *little* things for God; I turn the cake that is frying on the pan for the love of Him, and that done, if there is nothing else to call me, I prostrate myself in worship before Him, Who has given me grace to work; afterwards, I rise happier than a king. It is enough for me to pick up but a straw from the ground for the love of God."[4]

Two Feathers, too, has mastered the art of presenting each heart-rending incident to God in her high-stress job as a night-shift childcare worker. After each encounter, she responds in an endless series of reflective poems that she jots down while praying over each little life entrusted to her care through the long hours of the night.

And, finally, like Brother Lawrence, Teresa was granted her own M. Beaufort, a chronicler who has ordered several of her poems for us and contextualized them from Teresa's memories. As Teresa is calm and silent, her chronicler, Jeanne DeFazio, is all excitement. An actress of Spanish / Italian descent, straight out of Hollywood, she left the glitz and glamour of

---

3. Brother Lawrence, *Practice of the Presence*, 30.
4. Ibid., 90–91.

Introduction

a career of make-believe, playing supporting parts in movies and television series to take up a life of service to the marginalized in the drama of real life, as a teacher of second-language-learner children in the barrios of San Diego. A woman of great faith, intelligence, and energy, Jeanne responded to God's calling, pursuing seminary education at Gordon-Conwell Theological Seminary, and, after graduation, returned as an Athanasian Teaching Scholar at its multicultural Boston Center for Urban Ministerial Education (CUME), which serves the often unnoticed but thriving ethnic churches.

The result of these women's collaboration is a simple but uplifting example of how any of us, despite the sadness we must negotiate in this fallen world, can daily be filled, not with despair, but with gratitude to God, as moment by moment we can find relief, "having thrown all our concerns on Him, because we are of concern to Him."[5]

As M. Beaufort met Brother Lawrence and was blessed by that meeting, one of the reasons we read books is to meet interesting authors and hear something helpful that will enrich our own lives. In this brief book, you will meet two thoughtful, active, caring women who have drawn lessons from lives of rich experience that will enrich your own. Their little offering was designed as a kind of compact contemporary breviary, chronicling an ongoing conversation with God in the midst of caretaking suffering lives. This simple, accessible little devotional should be taken like a medicine in daily doses: repeat as necessary until your spirit is heartened. I was moved in my spirit and encouraged in my commitment to act by contemplating these lives and these prayers and I trust you will be too. Expect to be sobered, nourished, uplifted, and spurred to responsive action—in short: blessed and edified. I was.

—William David Spencer

William David Spencer is the author or editor of a dozen books, including *The Prayer Life of Jesus* and *Joy Through the Night: Biblical Resources for Suffering People*, both of which he co-authored with his wife, and the award-winning urban adventure novel, *Name in the Papers*. He is a volunteer founding pastor of Pilgrim Church of Beverly, MA, and a professor of theology at the Boston campus of Gordon-Conwell Theological Seminary.

5. 1 Peter 5:7, Translation by author.

While working with emotionally disturbed children in Massachusetts' state and private programs, Teresa Flowers began to journal her prayers. As an overnight supervisor, Teresa ensured the safety and well-being of children on the night shift. During those night watches, Teresa also journaled her conversations with God.

As an example, Teresa said the following prayer for a child from Rwanda whom she renamed Moses for inclusion in this book. He suffered nightmares from lying "dead" among corpses to keep from being killed during Rwanda's recent civil wars:

Listen to My Heartbeat

Listen to the beat of a child's heart,
Hear the cries of, "I'm lonely, scared;
I'm hungry for affection."
Listen to the beat of a child's heart:
"Rescue me from hell!"
Listen to the heart of a child's cry.

Teresa's prayers grew into an adventure. An attitude of gratitude in the challenges of everyday life began to fill Teresa's heart. She found appreciation for God when things were good and when things were bad. In that spirit of humble gratitude, God increased Teresa's portion.

She chose to share these prayers with you so that you too may enjoy an attitude of gratitude on the night shifts of your life.

Note: As a child, Teresa was the victim of abuse. Through the dark valley of her own painful childhood, Teresa brings a healing touch to those children who had been similarly wounded. In this prayer, Teresa wrote of "The Second Mile," expressing her vision to love and heal the hurting through Jesus' love and the power of the Holy Spirit.

Second Mile Walk

∽

God of ages has called me to the
Second Mile
To walk with my children through
the valley.
I pray for the strength and the good
courage to continue the walk,
To be there in the darkness,
to be there in the light,
The Second Mile is to be there.

The following are stories of children whom Teresa has renamed with names from the Bible to protect their innocence.

Rachel

Rachel was abandoned by her mom when she was five years old. Along with her two-year-old sister, she bounced from foster home to foster home until she came into Teresa's care on the night shift. When Rachel was angry, she would bite and her eyes would roll into the back of her head. After time spent in specific prayer for Rachel, Teresa began to see deliverance in the child's life. Rachel loved to cook, so she began to help Teresa prepare the Saturday morning breakfast club. In many dysfunctional homes, abuse commonly occurs at mealtimes. Teresa wrote "The Kitchen Prayer" about healing at mealtimes:

The Kitchen Prayer

∼

I thank You, Father, for the dirty pots
and pans in the sink,
You have allowed me to feed someone.
I thank You, Father, for the fellowship,
You have allowed me to befriend
someone.
I thank You, Father,
for the warmth of Your Love,
You have allowed me to share with
someone.
I thank You, Lord, for the smells in the
kitchen that draw people in,
You have allowed me to share Your Love.

Hannah

Hannah is a seven-year-old girl who came into Teresa's care after being sexually molested in her home environment. She would kick, bite, and run away when angry. Oftentimes, sexually abused children will carry memories of smells and sounds that plague them. As a healing for these memories of abuse, Teresa wrote "Smell of God" as a prayer for Hannah. As Teresa continued to spend time in prayer for her, Hannah became more confident and less in need of constant approval.

Smell of God

Smell the Purity of the Spirit,
Smell the Love,
Smell the Joy,
Smell the Peace,
Smell the Quietness of our Souls,
Smell God.

All the children Teresa cared for acted out because of painful memories of abuse and neglect. Teresa cried out to the Lord to heal these memories. The following prayer reflects a moment when Teresa stood in the gap for her emotionally shattered children:

I Stood

Lonely I stood before God
With a broken and shattered heart
Praying for a healing touch.
Through the pain and the hurtful suffering,
God's healing touch began a knitting together of the children's souls to His Spirit,
God put their hearts back together into perfect stained-glass windows.

In "Lonely Night of the Soul," Teresa expressed the spiritual promise of God within her. When the children battled, ran away, or lashed out at her, she called on "the strength of God that comes from deep within her":

Lonely Night of the Soul

When fears grip my thoughts,
I come face to face with the children's
pain,
Their lonely night of the soul.
Then the Lord's strength comes out from
deep within me
To battle the pain of their past with Love.

David

David's parents were unmarried. His father abandoned both David and his mom when David's mother became terminally ill. He was ten when he began to bounce from foster home to foster home. When he first came into Teresa's care, he would hiss like an animal. After Teresa prayed for him, David stopped hissing and became more peaceful.

As an offering of praise to God for David's healing, Teresa wrote "God's Interpretations." In this prayer, Teresa shares her sense of rebirth in the Holy Spirit when David's breakthroughs occurred.

God's Interpretations

Praise God for His interpretations
in our lives,
Praise God for His saving grace
interpretations,
Praise God for His interpretations:
The children's minds are renewed,
Praise God for His interpretations:
His Son's blood,
Praise God for His interpretations:
The children have clean hearts,
Praise God for His interpretations:
They are healed,
Praise God for His interpretations:
They are made whole,
Praise God, the children have been
interpreted.

Teresa has been on a journey with damaged youth. She experienced the love of God pouring into their bodies, souls, and spirits because of Jesus. These spiritual travels brought Teresa to make this petition before her Lord in prayer:

Make Them into Your Image, Make Them into Your Children

∼

Mold them through the refined fire,
Bring out the dross,
Send in Your love,
Make them a new creation.

Tamar

Tamar, who was prostituted by her mother for drugs and money, was a developmentally disabled child of 13 when she came under Teresa's care on the night shift. She clung to the male staff but would not speak to the female staff. After Teresa spent successive nights in prayer for Tamar, the following happened: Tamar climbed up a fence into a tree and got scared. Teresa found her, however, and she allowed Teresa to help her out of the tree. Teresa was grateful for the trust Tamar had put in her and thanked God for the breakthrough in the child's life.

Come to the Place

Come to the place where broken hearts
are mended;
Bodies are healed; minds are made
whole,
Bring them to the place where love
abounds,
Mercy flows as a river,
Bring them to the place
Where children are children,
Bring them to the place
Where love surrounds us all.

As Teresa opened up her eyes and ears and heart to hear from God, He spoke of His special love—His special love for abused and hurting children. In "Let Them Seek Your Face," Teresa pleads with Jesus to let the children seek His face.

Let Them Seek Your Face

∼

Let them seek Your face
So that You can wipe away their tears,
So that You can show them Your Love,
Let them seek Your face with their whole hearts,
Let them seek Your face.

Teresa was able to see growth and healing in her children's lives as she continued to journal prayers on the night shift. Her burdens lightened, and she was able to awaken with a prayer of praise and thanksgiving in her heart.

Morning Prayer

∼

Praise You, God,
Thank You for the miracle of life
that You gave me,
I can see the Son rising in my life,
I can hear You calling my name,
I can speak of Your love,
I can taste Your sweetness,
I can smell life.

As God healed the children's minds and hearts and souls, Teresa opened up to the love of Jesus calling her into His arms for comfort after a long night's work. "Perfect Our Hearts" expresses the healing power of the love of Jesus:

Perfect Our Hearts

Perfect our hearts with Your love,
Let us see Your love in our hearts,
Perfect our hearts with Your touch,
Let us feel Your love in our hearts,
Perfect our hearts with Your hand,
Let us feel Your healing touch.

Samuel

Samuel was adopted from a northern European orphanage by an American family. He fought with his American mother who gave him up to a foster home. He was wounded and full of abandonment issues. Teresa would plead the blood of Jesus over Samuel as he often woke up at night panicked from nightmares.

Teresa would often plead the blood of Jesus over her children's lives while in prayer to spiritually protect them. "Father of Their Souls" is Teresa's prayer to God, the Father of her children's souls:

Father of Their Souls

When the blood of Jesus washed
down on them,
tears of joy overcame me.
I worship You, my Father:
You are Father of the children's souls.
When the blood washed down on them,
I cried out with love to my Father.
"I worship You;
You are Father of the children's souls."
When the blood washed down on them,
I danced for You, Father of my soul.
When the blood washed down on them,
I praised You, Father of my soul.
Your love overcame them.

Samuel, David, Moses, Tamar, Hannah, Rachel, and so many other abused and hurting children came through the care of Teresa on the night shift. Teresa prayed these prayers for all the children when they were distressed, enraged, or conflicted:

When God's Children Pray

When God's children pray,
Strongholds are broken,
Healings are done, we are made whole,
Answers to prayers are seen everywhere.
He is here:
The blind see, the lame walk,
His presence is known,
He is here.

Quietness of Souls, the Holy Spirit Moves over Them

∼

Quietness of souls, the Holy Spirit
moves over them,
Meeting them where they are, opening
them up,
Sending the light to cleanse them,
Soothing their nerves, lifting them
up to the heavens,
Sounding waves of the Lord,
echoing through their minds,
Brilliance of light etching away the
darkness of sin,
Quietness of the Holy Spirit moves
over them.
Waves of love cleanse their souls,
Making them hungry for Your love.

As Teresa began to see the changes in herself and the children, she listened for God's guidance each night. In "Bring the Light to the Darkness of Their Hearts," Teresa asked Jesus to send the Holy Spirit to bring the children to Him:

Bring the Light to the Darkness of Their Hearts

Bring the light to the darkness of their hearts,
Bringing their hearts back to Your Word,
Bringing the Holy Spirit into their hearts,
Bringing them to their knees.

Cause Them to Seek You with Their Hearts

Cause them to seek You with their hearts,
Bowing down with their physical bodies.
Cause them to reach out to You with
their hearts.
Lift their hearts to praise You.
Grasp them in Your hands.
Hold them close to You.

I Am Silent Before You

∼

I am silent before You,
Waiting for You to answer.
Speak to their hearts.
May Your glory shine before the children.
Chase away the darkness.
Bring them close to You.
Make them one with You.
Amen.

Fire of the Lord

Fire of the Lord, all-consuming fire,
Fall upon them.
Cleanse them from the mire.
Burn up the pain of the past.
Make them transparent,
only seeing You now.

Let the Children Come and Worship You

Let the children come and worship You.
Let them dance and sing to You.
Let them walk with You.
Allow them to see in Your heart.
Let the children come and worship,
dancing and singing to You.
Bless them.
Anoint them.
Show them Your love.

Voice of the Holy Spirit, Speak Softly

Voice of the Holy Spirit, speak softly in
the children's ears of Your love for them.
As they dance their praises for You,
As they bow their heads to You,
As their eyes are lifted to Your face,
Let them hear Your voice in their ears,
The Voice of the Holy Spirit.
Speak to their souls, giving them the
spark of life.

Your Touch Has Caressed Their Souls

Your touch has caressed their souls.
Your hand has opened up their hearts.
Your Spirit has touched their inner beings.
Your eyes have sought them.
Your blood has bought them.
They are Yours.

May the Blessings of the Lord Be upon the Children

∼

May the blessings of the Lord be upon
the children.
May the breath of the Lord God
be in the children.
May His spirit guide them.
May His eye be upon them.
May the unspoken prayers of their
hearts be answered.

You Know

~

You know, God my Father, You know
what is best for the children.
You know when they need Your touch.
You know when they need a shoulder to
cry on.
You know them when they don't know
themselves.

As Teresa continued in prayer for the children, she received this vision:

On Eagles' Wings of Love

∼

I can see beyond the tomorrow
of this world,
Into the heavens' healing of these
children's souls,
When no more darkness surrounds them.

Are you on the night shift of your life?
Do you feel abandoned like Rachel?
Do you feel abused like Hannah?
Do you feel angry like David?
Do you feel afraid like Tamar?
Do you feel heartbroken like Samuel?
Turn your heart to Jesus.
He will heal you with His love,
and give you an attitude of gratitude!

For more information contact:

Jeanne DeFazio
Post Office Box 72081
Davis, CA 95617

jcdefazio55@gmail.com

www.ingramcontent.com/pod-product-compliance
Lightning Source LLC
Chambersburg PA
CBHW061313040426
42444CB00010B/2626